OFF TO THE REVOLUTION

OFF TO THE REVOLUTION

MORE CARTOONS BY PAT OLIPHANT

Andrews and McMeel
A Universal Press Syndicate Company
Kansas City

Oliphant® is distributed internationally by Universal Press Syndicate.

ISBN: 0-8362-0429-8

Library of Congress Catalog Card Number: 95-79086

June 29, 1994

WHERE'D EVERYBODY GO?

THEY CALLED THE STAFF IN TO MEET MR. PANETTA. 'THIS,' HE THOUGHT, 'AIN'T GONNA BE EASY.'

June 30, 1994

OLIPHANT
LOBBYIST
LEGAL BILLS
MY GOD! BIMBOS, SIR— THEY KNOW YOU CAN'T RESIST THEM!

'THE GIRLS TOOK UP A COLLECTION, HON—NO STRINGS ATTACHED.'

MERELY A SUMMER SHOWER

CONGRESS, (ALREADY WELL PROTECTED, THANKYOU) PONDERS THE HEALTH CARE NEEDS OF THE GREAT UNWASHED.

July 4, 1994

THE SEARCH WARRANT IS IN THE MAIL

'BEATS ME — I SUPPOSE IT'S THE L.A.P.D. ON THE TRAIL OF HOT EVIDENCE.'

July 6, 1994

YASSIR ARAFAT TAKES A DESK JOB.

July 7, 1994

DARK ANGELS OF THE RIGHT.

July 8, 1994

WHY WAIT FOR SUPPERTIME WHEN YOU CAN START EATING NOW?

July 9, 1994

NOW THEY'RE WIDE AWAKE!

'.. AND SO WE MUST PONDER THE EVERLASTING MYSTERY, THE ETERNAL QUESTION. AND ON THE ANSWER HINGES, PERHAPS, THE FATE OF OUR WORLD... DID, OR DID NOT, O. J. DO IT?'

July 9, 1994

'DON'T STRUGGLE, THEY SAY. DON'T FIGHT IT. JUST BE STILL AND WAIT FOR HELP TO ARRIVE. DON'T PANIC...'

July 30, 1994

BUS STOP
NICE OUTFIT, HUSSEIN
YOU, TOO, YITZHAK - WHAT'S ON THE AGENDA?
THAT'S AN ODD COUPLE

TRUE STATESMANSHIP COMES IN MANY GUISES.

July 30, 1994

RWANDA
WAIT—DID YOU NOTICE THAT BACK THERE?
YES, I SUPPOSE I DID.
WELL, DON'T YOU THINK WE SHOULD GO BACK AND HELP?
I DON'T KNOW—WE MAY GET INVOLVED. REMEMBER SOMALIA. AND HAITI. I MEAN, THESE PEOPLE SEEM TO DO THIS ALL THE TIME... DIE IN THE ROAD, THAT IS.
WELL, MAYBE WE SHOULD HELP, ANYWAY.
YOU COULD BE RIGHT, I EXPECT...

July 30, 1994

U.S. POSTAL SERVICE
U.S. POSTAL SERVICE
U.S. POSTAL SERVICE
U.S. POSTAL SERVICE

August 3, 1994

INVASION
DEMOCRAC
HOW WILL THIS HELP ME?
U.N.
HAITI
WELL, IF YOU SURVIVE THE REMEDY, WE GIVE YOU THE CURE!

'READY?'

August 4, 1994

MARRIED!!
THE JACKSONS
MICHAEL, LISA MARIE JACKSON!
HEY, IT'S A LONG, SLOW SUMMER..
OLIPHANT

'YOU MEDIA PEOPLE ARE SO DARN DETERMINED TO TURN THIS INTO A FREAK SHOW, I REALLY JUST DON'T KNOW WHAT TO DO... NO, MR. JACKSON DOESN'T REALLY KNOW WHAT TO DO, EITHER...'

August 5, 1994

ABORTION CLINIC
HOURS
BLESSED ARE THE SELF-RIGHTEOUS, FOR THEY ARE ALWAYS RIGHT
KILL A BABY KILLER FOR JESUS
OLIPHANT

'SIMPLY EXERCISIN' MY RIGHT OF FREE SPEECH!'

August 6, 1994

HANG ON FOR THE BUMP, MR. ALTMAN!
OOPS!
OH, WELL... I'M BEHIND YOU ONE THOUSAND PERCENT, MR. ALTMAN...
JEEZ, I GOTTA GET SOME DISTANCE BETWEEN ME AND THIS GUY!

August 10, 1994

I GAVE HIM YOUR MESSAGE THAT WITH REGARD TO HEALTH CARE, YOU WOULD ACCEPT NOTHING LESS THAN TOTAL VICTORY. HE SAID THAT SOUNDED FINE TO HIM.
THEN, LET'S MUDDLE THROUGH TO VICTORY. SHALL WE?
Senate

August 11, 1994

HELPING THE PENTAGON WATCH FOR RUSSIANS, IF IT'S ANY OF YOUR DAM' BUSINESS!
NATIONAL RECONNAISSANCE OFFICE
A DIVISION OF ROCKWELL INTERNATIONAL
THE PRICE OF VIGILANCE IS ETERNAL
THE BILL $8 BILLION $8,000,000,000

August 12, 1994

WHATEVER DO YOU THINK WILL BECOME OF MR. CLINTON?
WELL, A LEADER HE AIN'T. HE HAS NO SUPPORT IN CONGRESS SO HE CAN'T EXPECT, TO GET HIS UNIVERSAL COVERAGE HEALTH PLAN APPROVED...
THEN, ALONG WITH HIS WHITE-WATER TROUBLES, HE'S FOREVER BEING AMBUSHED BY BIMBOS AND MOUTHY RIGHT-WING JESUS FOLKS..
NO WAITER IN THE WORLD COULD EVER GET HIS ORDER STRAIGHT BECAUSE HE CHANGES HIS MIND EVERY MINUTE...
NO FIRM IN ITS RIGHT MIND WOULD EVER HIRE THE ARROGANT NINNIES HE CALLS AIDES...
HE CAN'T GET ALONG WITH THE MEDIA...
AND HE HAS NO MONOLITHIC THREAT TO RALLY US AGAINST, OTHER THAN JURASSIC-ERA REPUBLICANS.
THAT ALL MEANS I'M A ONE-TERM FIRST CAT, DON'T IT?
LOOK AT THE UPSIDE...
NO MORE AUGUSTS IN WASHINGTON.

August 12, 1994

OR WOULD
THEY CARE?

IF THE OWNERS AND PLAYERS MOONED A TOTALLY EMPTY STADIUM, WOULD IT MAKE A DIFFERENCE?

August 17, 1994

August 18, 1994

WANTED

Noted Con Man & Republican Thug
'Nasty Newt' Gingrich

for acts of thuggery, muggery, disruption & senseless mayhem. Passes himself off as devout supporter of law and order, but carries assault weapon. Long past the 'Three Strikes, You're Out' limit, faces max. sentence when caught.

IF CAUGHT!

August 19, 1994

WHAT NOW???!
— LET ME REVIEW THAT @!!?** CUBAN ADJUSTMENT ACT OF 1966!
WHERE DID WE PUT THE 'GO AWAY' MAT?
NO HABLO EENGLES

August 22, 1994

WE CAN'T SAVE HIM SO WE'LL HAVE TO SHOOT HIM... AGREED?
AGREED, BUT MY HANDS ARE NOT STEADY.. YOU DO IT.
I'D BE HAPPY TO DO IT, BUT I'M NOT TAKING THE RAP FOR IT!
NEITHER AM I – YOU DO IT!
I ALREADY HAVE HEALTH COVERAGE, BESIDES, YOU'RE A BETTER SHOT THAN I AM – YOU DO IT...
MAYBE WE COULD ALL SHOOT HIM, THEN NOBODY DID IT...
UNIVERSAL HEALTH CARE
FACED WITH THE COURAGE OF THEIR UNCONVICTIONS.

August 24, 1994

OLIPHANT
WHOMP
THUD
STAMP
TROMP
CRIME BILL
SHEESH - THAT WAS NEARLY A ONE-STOMP-YOU'RE-OUT!
OK, SOON HE'S GOIN' TO TRY COMIN' BACK ON THROUGH WITH HIS DAM' HEALTH CARE BILL....

August 24, 1994

WHAT THEN, FIDEL? AFTER WE HAVE OVERTHROWN THE UNITED STATES AND FREED THE PEOPLE? WHAT THEN?
DAM'!! I'LL HAVE TO GET TOUGH WITH THESE PEOPLE— OBVIOUSLY THEY'RE TRYING TO OVERTHROW THE UNITED STATES!
SOMEBODY TELL EVERY-BODY ABOUT THE COMMIE MENACE!

August 26, 1994

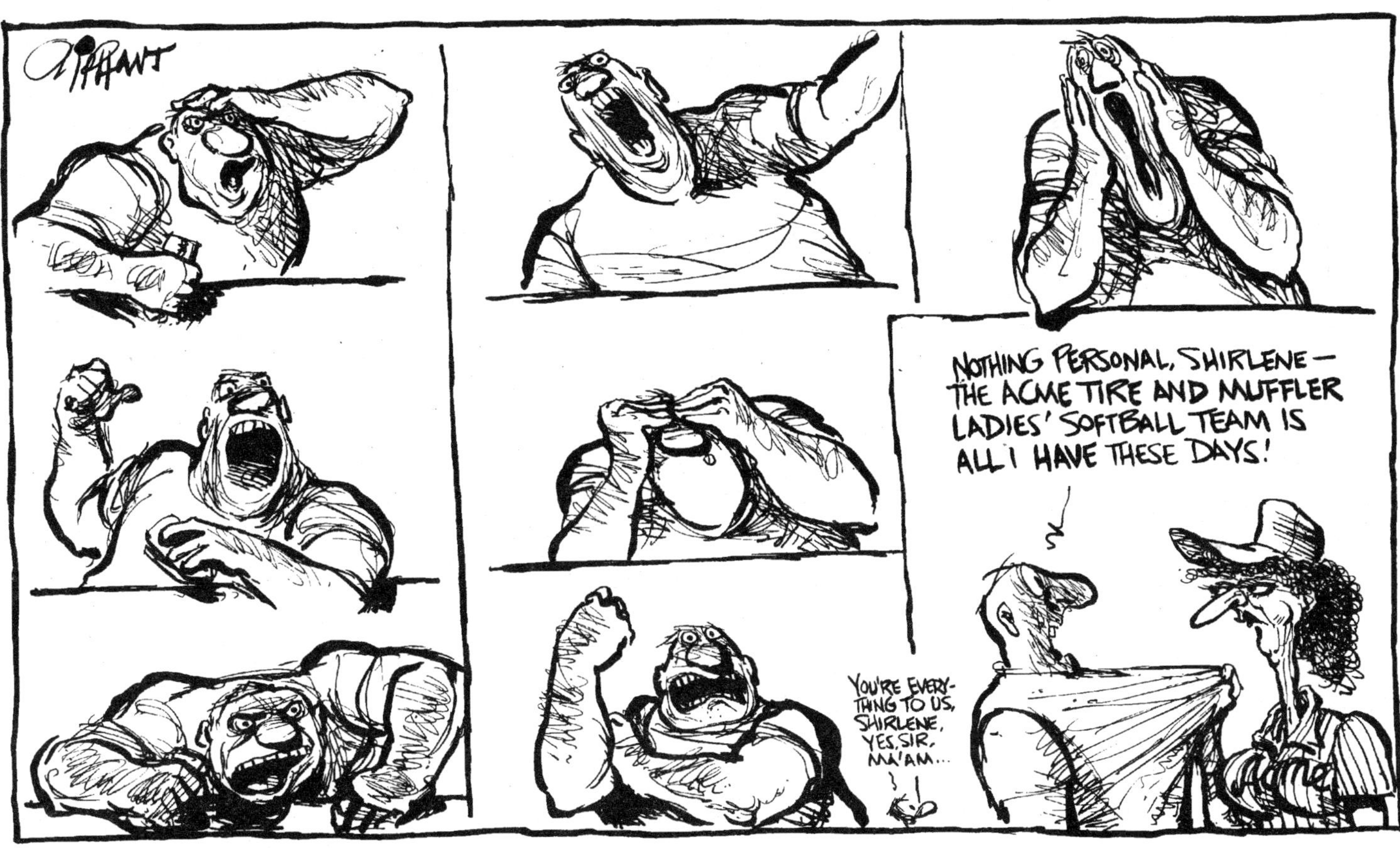
OLIPHANT
NOTHING PERSONAL, SHIRLENE— THE ACME TIRE AND MUFFLER LADIES' SOFTBALL TEAM IS ALL I HAVE THESE DAYS!
YOU'RE EVERYTHING TO US, SHIRLENE, YES, SIR, MA'AM...
ACME

August 27, 1994

COULD THEY BE TRYING TO LOSE US?
HEALTH CARE

'WHERE'D EVERYBODY GO?'

August 31, 1994

September 1, 1994

HAITI
NEXT TO THE "BUSINESS AS USUAL" SIGN?

'PUT A SIGN IN THE WINDOW—"BACK IN 30 YEARS"!'

September 2, 1994

SIT DOWN, WHOY DON'T YOU? IF YOU'LL SIT DOWN, THEN OI'LL SIT DOWN, THEN WE'LL BE ALL SITTIN' DOWN.
OI'LL SIT DOWN WHIN OI'M GOOD N' READY, NOT BECAUSE IT WAS YOU TELLIN' ME TO... NOW, YOU SIT DOWN FIRST.
IRISH PEACE TALKS
IF THE ISRAELIS CAN SIT DOWN WITH THE PALESTINIANS, WHY SHOULDN'T THESE TWO?..
BECAUSE THEIR NAMES WEREN'T O'PERES AND McARAFAT, THAT'S WHY!
OLIPHANT

September 4, 1994

NOLO CONTRACEPTIUM
IS THIS THE HOLY SEE?
RATHER IT'S THE HOLY 'NOW HEAR THIS'

'IT'S NOT GRABBING THEM, HOLINESS — PERHAPS WE SHOULD JUST STICK WITH SIMPLER ORDERS LIKE "NO MEAT ON FRIDAYS"...'

September 7, 1994

WHY DO THEY NEED A CONFERENCE ON WORLD OVERPOPULATION WHEN THEY HAVE US?
WAR
FAMINE
PESTILENCE
DISEASE
OLIPHANT

September 7, 1994

THE SEARCH FOR AN IMPARTIAL JUROR
AT LAST!!
FIRST, A SIMPLE TEST..
KNOCK KNOCK
WHO'S THERE?
O.J.
GUILTY, O.J.

September 9, 1994

IT'S THE POPE ON LINE ONE. HE'S DEMANDING TO SPEAK TO YOU. HE'S DEMANDING YOU GET THE ABORTION WORDING CHANGED IN THE POPULATION CONFERENCE RESOLUTION. HE DEMANDS YOU ACT AT ONCE AND HE WON'T TAKE NO FOR AN ANSWER. HE SAYS HE KNOWS WHAT YOU WANT AND HE'S GONNA GET IT FOR YOU. HE....
TELL HIM I'M OUT
(SIGH)
MAYBE WHAT I WANT IS A WOMAN POPE..
WAITING ROOM
HIMSELF IS
IN
COULDN'T HURT

September 10, 1994

JUST WHEN YOU THOUGHT IT WAS SAFE TO GO BACK IN THE VOTING BOOTH...

September 14, 1994

'STAY OUT OF THE WHITE HOUSE AIR SPACE — THE SECRET SERVICE HAS SOMETHING TO PROVE.'

September 15, 1994

CONGRESS WAS UNANIMOUS ON THIS ONE

LATE BULLETIN – WASHINGTON: INSTEAD OF GOING TO HAITI, THE U.S. TASK FORCE IS MOVING UP THE POTOMAC AT THIS HOUR TO SAVE THE CRIPPLED CITY FROM MARION BARRY.

September 16, 1994

HEY, SOCKS – WHAT DID YOU THINK OF MR. CLINTON'S SPEECH?
WELL, IT'S LIKE I SAID TO HIM, LOOK, I SAID, IF YOU THINK THAT HAITIAN MESS...
HEY- THANKS
IS WORTH ONE AMERICAN LIFE, AND IF YOU THINK THAT'S WHAT YOU HAVE TO DO...
TO GET RE-ELECTED, THEN BY ALL MEANS GO AHEAD! INVADE!
YECCH
I SUPPOSE THE COMMANDER-IN-CHIEF PLANS TO LEAD THE FIRST WAVE UP THE BEACH?
I THINK HE PLANS TO GO TO CANADA SOMEPLACE

September 17, 1994

BUT WHERE COULD WE FIND VOTERS THAT STUPID?
I THINK I KNOW WHERE YOU COULD START LOOKING

'I'VE GOT AN IDEA FOR '96— I GO BACK, I BEG FORGIVENESS, PLAY THE WHOLE REDEMPTION BIT, THE REFORMED UNDERDOG BACK FROM HELL, I GET RE-ELECTED, WE TAKE OVER...'

September 21, 1994

DRAT!
THANKS, JIMMY.
Y'ALL WEKK'M ANY TIME
GEN. CÉDRAS HAS YOUR WATCH AND YOUR CREDIT CARDS, JIMMY
ARISTIDE

September 22, 1994

JOIN THE ARMY
GOOD BENEFITS
FREE UNIFORM
BE ALL OUR POLICY WILL ALLOW YOU TO BE
U.S.
TRAVEL TO EXOTIC LANDS
MAKE NEW FRIENDS
HEY
WATCH THE LOCAL POLICE BEAT THEM TO DEATH
BE UNABLE TO INTERVENE
WELCOME TO HAITI
PONDER THE POINT OF IT ALL.

THAT SLANDERS WOLVES
AND SHEEP
RIGHT WING EXTREMIST
CENTRIST

A WOLF, IN ANY OTHER GUISE, IS STILL PAT ROBERTSON.

September 25, 1994

HELP
SOON I MAY LOSE MY ANTI TRUST EXEMPTION
OWNER
Players
Help
Soon i may HAV To go WERK FOR a Living
BAD DOG! VERY BAD DOG! OH, THOSE POOR PEOPLE - DON'T YOU EVER DO THAT AGAIN!
TOO OFTEN...
WELL TRAINED PUPPY, THAT

September 28, 1994

'FAR TOO HIGH-RISK—CANCEL HIS POLICY.'

September 29, 1994

REAGANISM
WHERE DID THEY DIG THAT UP?
OLIPHANT

THE GINGRICH CONTRACT.

September 30, 1994

OPRAH? FOR ME?
I CAN'T WAIT FOR PEOPLE MAGAZINE TO CALL
I THINK I SHOULD GET AN AGENT
I WONDER WHAT ONE SHOULD CHARGE FOR AN INTERVIEW...
THIS IS SUCH FUN – I'VE NEVER BEEN A CELEBRITY BEFORE
HONEY, THAT JUDGE TURNS OFF THE TV CAMERAS, AIN'T NO USE IN ANY OF THIS.
MR. DONOHUE?! WHY, YES, I AM AVAILABLE
GUILTY OR NOT, WE'RE GONNA GIVE HIM A FAIR TRIAL – KNOWWADDI MEAN?
I KNOW HE'S INNOCENT – I JUST KNOW IT.
HE'S AT LEAST EIGHTY PERCENT INNOCENT
WE BETTER FIND HIM INNOCENT OR WE GONNA HAVE SOME BAAAAD RIOTS
I THINK I SHOULD BE IN THE PRESS SECTION...
HAVE YOU REACHED A VERDICT?
WE FIND THIS IS A REAL TRIP!

WE, THE JURY.

October 1, 1994

I WOULDN'T WORRY ABOUT IT — THE PRESIDENCY IS A JOB Y'ALL HAVE TO GROW INTO.
SOME OF Y'ALL DO.
SOME OF Y'ALL NEVER WILL.

October 5, 1994

STAR SPANGLED BANNER
RE-ELECT FREDDY FUDD
DOG CATCHER
THE END OF A PROMISING POLITICAL CAREER
WHOSE?

THEN THE PRESIDENT CAME TO HELP FREDDY WITH HIS CAMPAIGN...

October 6, 1994

HONEY, WITH YOUR MONEY AND MY AMBITION WE CAN REALLY GO PLACES
GET RIGHT UP CLOSE TO THE SUN, THERE, SIR

ICARUS HUFFINGTON AND HIS UPWARDLY MOBILE GREEK

October 8, 1994

THE NEW AMERICAN SEX STUDY SAYS THIRTY PERCENT OF THE COUPLES SURVEYED HAVE IT ONCE A YEAR.
TARNATION! NOW I SUPPOSE YOU'LL BE DEMANDIN' IT EVERY DURN YEAR!
ONCE A YEAR! THEN HOW COME YOU'RE SMILING?
TODAY'S THE DAY!
OLIPHANT

October 12, 1994

ALL THE IMPORTANTLY IMPORTANT MINDS OF WASHINGTON HAVE PONDERED AND EXPOUNDED AND EXPANDED ON THE TIMING OF MY LATEST MOVE, MISSING, ALL THE WHILE, THE SIMPLEST EXPLANATION..
HEY, I'M AN ARMED AND DANGEROUS LUNATIC —
TIMING HAS NOTHING TO DO WITH IT.
CNN
POOR SADDAM - HE HAD TO CATCH YOU ON A RESOLUTE DAY!
OLIPHANT
IT'S AN ILL WIND, HOWEVER, DOESN'T BLOW SOMEBODY SOME GOOD.
Dear Saddam, Thankyou, thankyou, oh, thank you, thankyou thankyou

October 13, 1994

NO ONE REALLY KNOWS WHAT HAPPENED TO GEN. CEDRAS AFTER HE LEFT HAITI. BUT, JUST YESTERDAY, ON A LONELY FREIGHT PLATFORM IN RURAL GEORGIA, A CRATE WAS DELIVERED...
PLAINS GA
TO JIMMY CARTER PLAINS, GA
CONTENTS - SUNDAY SCHOOL TEACHER & WIFE
FREIGHT

FORKED TONGUE
OLLIE SNAKE
Serpentus Northus
VENOMOUS & DANGEROUS
HABITAT: FAR RIGHT VIRGINIA
TREAD ON ME
LORD! THE THINGS THEY ALLOW TO RUN THESE DAYS!
NOT RUN-SLITHER

October 15, 1994

'UNEMPLOYMENT IS BELOW 6 PERCENT...'
'INFLATION IS 3 PERCENT...'
'THE FEDERAL DEFICIT'S DOWN...'
'SO FAR, SO GOOD IN BOTH HAITI AND THE GULF...'
WAITING FOR THE TIDE?
'SO WHY AM I HERE..?'

October 19, 1994

PEACE PRIZE CLUB
BACK DOOR CHAPTER
DR. KISSINGER, I PRESUME.
VHY, VELCOM, MR. ARAFAT
BLOOD BROTHERS, WE PRESUME

October 20, 1994

HOW GOES THE TRIAL, JUDGE ITO?
BETTER YOU DON'T ASK.
SLUDGE
'BETTER YOU SHOULD ASK, 'HOW GOES THE SLUDGE, JUDGE?'

October 20, 1994

IT'S CLOSE TO HALLOWEEN— SAY SOMETHIN' SCARY
MAYOR MARION BARRY!
GOTCHA
D.C. SCARES DON'T COUNT— GIMME ANOTHER ONE
OK— SENATOR HUFFINGTON!
GOTCHA AGIN!
NOW YOU TRY TO SCARE ME
SENATOR NORTH!!
IS SLIMY CUNNING A FORM OF INTELLIGENCE?
AND WHERE ARE THOSE FOLKS ON THE BELL CURVE?

October 22, 1994

MY OPPONENT IS A LOUSY, PHILANDERING LIAR OF DOUBTFUL PARENTAGE AND EVEN MORE DOUBTFUL ABILITY, AND ANTI-GOD AND UNAMERICAN, TOO!
YEAH?
YEAH!
MY OPPONENT IS A NO-GOOD, STINKIN' POLECAT WITH THE MANNERS OF A JACKAL AND THE INTELLIGENCE TO MATCH HIS UGLY APPEARANCE, AND A GODDAM BIGOT AS WELL!
HOW DO YOU VOTE WHEN YOU THINK THEY'RE BOTH RIGHT?
CAN'T THEY ADDRESS THE ISSUES?
THESE ARE THE ISSUES
OLIPHANT

November 2, 1994

ENTER QUIETLY
NO SUDDEN MOVEMENTS, NO EYE CONTACT

ON THE '94 CAMPAIGN TRAIL WITH PRESIDENT CLINTON — AT THE END OF THE DAY, THE SECRET SERVICE ENJOYS HAPPY HOUR.

November 3, 1994

November 5, 1994

SENATOR OLLIE?
SOME PEOPLE SAY I HAVE SOME DIFFICULTY WITH THE TRUTH
OR THEY SAY I'M A STRAIGHT-OUT LIAR.
AND A CHEAP DEMAGOGUE DEALING IN SIMPLISTIC NON-ISSUES.
AND THAT I LACK INTEGRITY
WELL
I'D SAY I'M PERFECTLY QUALIFIED FOR CONGRESS

November 7, 1994

OLIPHANT
HENCEFORTH, THE BULLY'S PULPIT.

THE SPEAKER'S CHAIR.

November 8, 1994

SIMPSON CIRCUS
HEY, IT BEATS WATCHING POLITICIANS!

'TAKE THE CAMERAS OUT OF THE COURTROOM?? WHAT ABOUT THE PUBLIC'S RIGHT TO BE ENTERTAINED?'

November 9, 1994

NOW LET'S SEE YOU RE-INVENT GOVERNANCE.

'I CAME TO OFFICE PROMISING TO RE-INVENT GOVERNMENT AND, BY GOLLY, I HAVE!'

November 10, 1994

YOU'RE PROBABLY WONDERING WHY WE CALLED THIS MEETING...
UM.. NOT REALLY
PROGRAM
PROGRAM
PROGRAM

November 11, 1994

WORDS FROM THE COMMON GROUND

'LET ME OFFER A CONCILIATORY HAND...'

November 16, 1994

BOBNEWT AIR
PRINC
LIGHT
HOLD TIGHT TO THAT CONTRACT!

'WHADDAYAKNOW! OUR OWN COMMUTER AIRLINE ... WHICH THE HELL IS THE 'ON' SWITCH?'

November 18, 1994

LISSEN... MR. GINGRICH WOULD LIKE YOU TO PRAY IN SCHOOL, AND, GOLLY, I HAVE NO REAL OBJECTION TO THAT... DO YOU?..
GOD SAVE US
AMEN

NOT TO MENTION THE MUGGERS AND MARION BARRY...

'BUT IT'S NOT ALL THAT LONELY, REALLY. NEWT COMES BY TO GLOAT EVERY DAY. AND, JESSE HELMS DROPPED BY TO THREATEN ME. SO I CAN'T SAY I WANT FOR COMPANY...'

November 23, 1994

LOOK AT THAT! A STRONG AND APPROPRIATE ACTION
STRONG? WHY, Y'ALL AIN'T FIT TO BE THE COMMANDER-IN-CHIEF!
TAKE THAT, YOU WICKED SERB, YOU!
NATO
BIP
DID HE GET THE MESSAGE YET?
THE SERB HEARD JESSE, - YES!
OLIPHANT

November 24, 1994

LEFTOVER TURKEY.

November 30, 1994

OF COURSE, WHEN YOU CONSIDER ALL THIS VICIOUS MURDER, AND SNIPING, AND SHELLING, AND MAIMING, AND KILLING FROM THE SERB POSITION...
...YOU HAVE TO CONCEDE THEY DO HAVE A POINT.
THE POINT IS, THEY WON.

SMOKELESS CIGARETTES WILL BE WILLINGLY SUPPLIED BY THE MANAGEMENT
DEFINITELY AN IDEA WHOSE TIME HAS COME

December 2, 1994

GUARANTEED MAIL DELIVERY
COMPETITIVE RATES
HOW'S THE SERVICE?
BETTER THAN THOSE BUMS IN THE POSTAL SERVICE

December 4, 1994

GATT
WHERE DOES JUMBO SIT?
ANYWHERE HE LIKES!

'HOWEVER, SOME ACKNOWLEDGMENTS ARE IN ORDER...'

December 8, 1994

HUBBELL
GOLLEE - WITH FRIENDS LIKE THIS...
IT'S OK - HE'S USED TO BEING TROD ON BY ELEPHANTS

'OOPS! JEEZ, SORRY, MR. PRESIDENT...'

December 9, 1994

FEDERAL
RESERVE
%
HEY, CLAUS - YOU GOT A CHUNK OF COAL FOR THIS GUY?

December 10, 1994

MRS. ARAFAT IS EXPECTING
WEINBERG
DELICATESSEN
YOU MUST MISS YOUR LIFE AS A SIMPLE TERRORIST

"...SO I SAID TO HER, 'THE INN'S CLOSED, EVERYTHING'S CLOSED — WHERE AM I GOING TO GET YOU KOSHER DILL PICKLES AT THREE IN THE MORNING, F'GODSAKE?'"

December 13, 1994

Y'KNOW, I CANNOT UNDERSTAND WHY MR. CLINTON FIRED JOYCELYN ELDERS!
SOCKS, TIMING IS EVERYTHING, AND SHE WAS TOTALLY OUT OF SYNC.
HEY! ALL SHE DID WAS MENTION SOMETHING THAT THIS HERE ADMINISTRATION HAS BEEN DOING SINCE IT CAME TO OFFICE!
YOU GOT ME THAT TIME
MAN! I OUGHTA REALLY CHEW HIM OUT FOR THIS!
WHUMP
CHEW??
WANT ADS
EMPLOYMENT
OH, YOU MEAN MASTICATION?
WHATEVER - I'M JUST A SIMPLE, ONE-TERM CAT FROM ARKANSAS

December 14, 1994

'..AND YOU BLOODY AMERICANS ARE JUST NOT DOING YOUR SHARE!'

December 15, 1994

'KISS ME,' SAID THE ONE FROG, 'AND I'LL TURN INTO A HANDSOME PRINCE!'
SO THE MIDDLECLASS MAIDEN KISSED HIM, AND FOOF!...
HE TURNED INTO NEWT GINGRICH!
THANKS— I'M GONNA TAX CUT!
FOR THAT GIVE YOU A
'KISS ME,' SAID THE OTHER FROG, 'AND I'LL TURN INTO A PRESIDENT!'
'BUT WHAT SORT OF A PRESIDENT?' ASKED THE MAIDEN, 'LIKE, I MEAN, WHO ARE YOU, REALLY? WHAT WOULD YOU STAND FOR?'
HEY! YOU WANT A TAX CUT? HECK, I'LL GIVE YOU A TAX CUT, PLUS A CAPITAL GAINS TAX CUT, PLUS TERM LIMITS!
ANYBODY SEE A PRINCE AROUND HERE?
OLIPHANT

December 16, 1994

NOW, I DON'T WANT YOU TOBACCO BOYS TO WORRY ABOUT A THING— I KNOW YOU WOULDN'T SELL ANYTHING ADDICTIVE.. HAW! WHY, HECK, YOU'D TELL ME IF IT WAS, WOULDN'T YOU? HAR!
PERJURY CHARGES
CLICK
HAW! HAK! CHOKE

OLIPHANT
PEACE IN YO' TIME
Signed: Jimmy Carter
MORE MESSIANIC, MR. CARTER.. THAT'S IT
CLICK

'IN JUST A LITTLE CLOSER TO MR. KARADZIC, MR. CARTER... THAT'S IT—SMILE' (CLICK)

December 22, 1994

SOCKS, THERE SEEMS TO BE A LOT OF GUNPLAY ROUND HERE OF LATE
WELL, THE WHITE HOUSE IS A MAGNET FOR DING-DONGS AND WEIRDOS.
INSIDE AND OUT.
I FEEL VERY GRATEFUL FOR THE ALERTNESS OF THE WONDERFUL OFFICERS OUTSIDE THE GATES.
WHY, ONLY YESTERDAY SOME SUSPICIOUS BEARDED GALOOT IN A RED SUIT APPROACHED THE FENCE, CARRYING A BIG SACK.
WHAT HAPPENED?
THE PARK POLICE DID THE ONLY PRUDENT THING— THEY SHOT HIM.

December 23, 1994

'IS THIS A GREAT COUNTRY, OR WHAT?'

December 24, 1994

THIS LOOKS LIKE A JOB FOR CARTERMAN - MAY I BE OF HEP?
Players
OWNERS
WHAT'S THE DIFFERENCE BETWEEN THE SERBS AND THE BASEBALL MOB?
YOU CAN REASON WITH THE SERBS

December 28, 1994

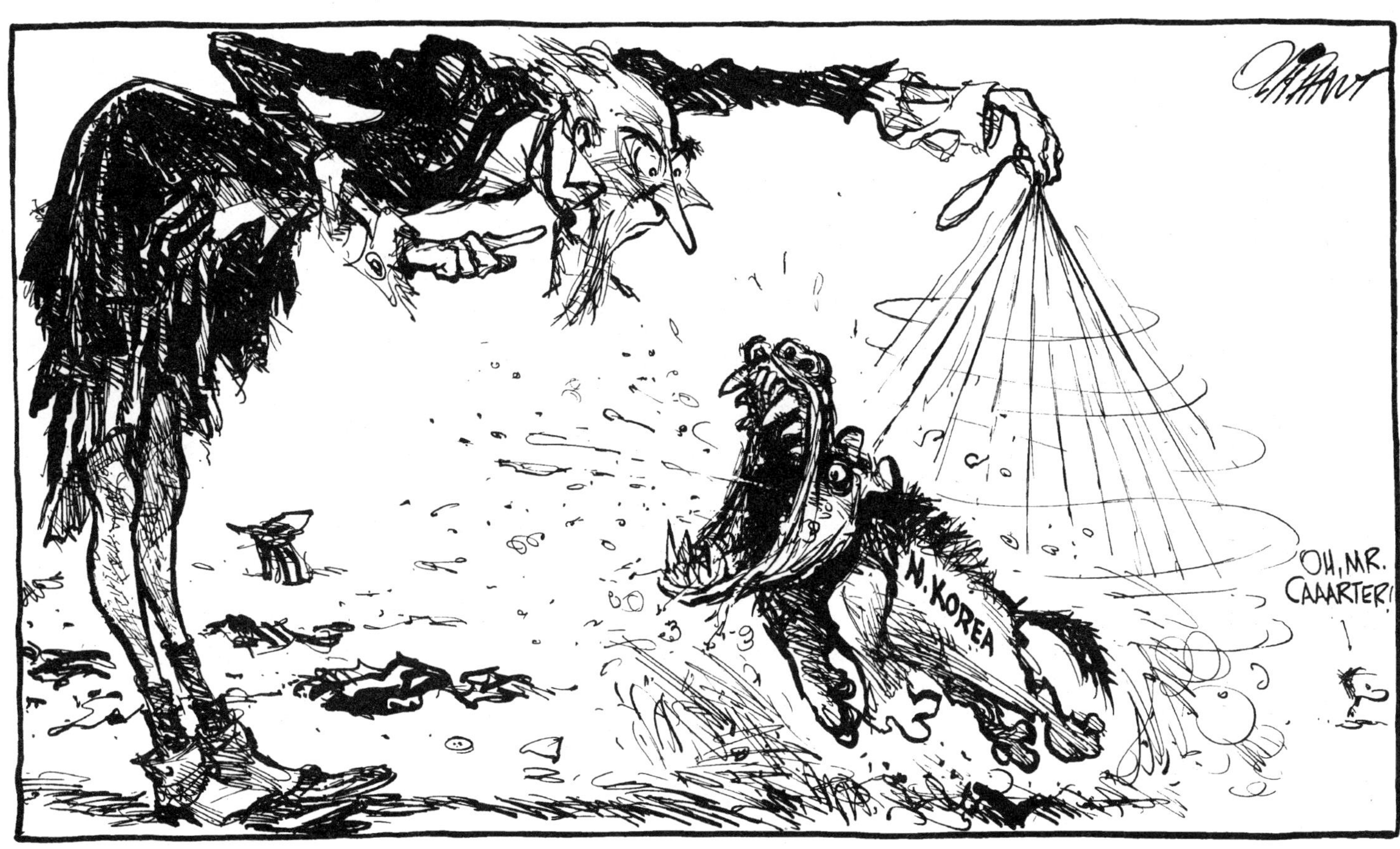
N. KOREA
OH, MR. CAAARTER!

December 29, 1994

PART OF
THE PEACE
DIVIDEND,
NO DOUBT

COP-KILLER BULLETS: WHAT'S A POOR, STARVING, OUT-OF-WORK, TOTALLY AMORAL DEFENSE INDUSTRY RESEARCH CHEMIST TO DO?

December 30, 1994

CIA
IN
HEY! WHO TH' HELL WAZZAT?
THAT? WHY THAT WAZZA DIRECTOR
HERE'S TO TH' DIRECTOR, GOD BLESS'M
TH' DIRECTOR IS DEAD, LONG LIVE TH' DIRECTOR
CIA
OUT
SLAM
WOOLSEY
WAS THAT THE WINDS OF CHANGE?
OLIPHANT

IS THIS AGENCY REALLY NECESSARY? (PART II).

January 1, 1995

.. AND, KID, ALWAYS MIND THE ADVICE OF YOUR ELDERS!
THAT WOULD BE JOYCELYN, I GUESS..
YOU HOPE
LET'S ASK IF SHE HAS A BOOK OUT.
FREE ADVICE FOR LIFE'S JOURNEY
1995

VODKA
MEDICINAL USE ONLY
CHECHEN NIGHT READING
AH WILL NOT SEEK, NOR WILL AH ACCEPT, MY PARTY'S NOMINATION, ETC...
LBJ
OLIPHANT

'BORIS, WHY DON'T Y'ALL DECLARE A VICTORY AND GO HOME?'

January 6, 1995

OH, I HATE THIS TUNE! CAN'T WE PLAY SOMETHING WE KNOW? HEY, YOU GUYS- LET'S CUT THE PACE A LITTLE! MY FEET HURT. DO WE HAVE TO MARCH ALL DAY AND ALL NIGHT? LET'S TRY A WALTZ, GUYS. WHAT KINDA REVOLUTION IS THIS? WHEN'S OUR FREE LUNCH? MY FEET HURT. OH, I HATE THIS TUNE!
OLIPHANT
JUST WHINE YANKEE-DOODLE

OFF TO THE REVOLUTION.

January 7, 1995

AH! TOWARDS RICHER DIALOGUE BETWEEN THE PARTIES
OH, YEAH? SHE DOES NOT, TOO, WEAR ARMY BOOTS, HILLARY!

January 11, 1995

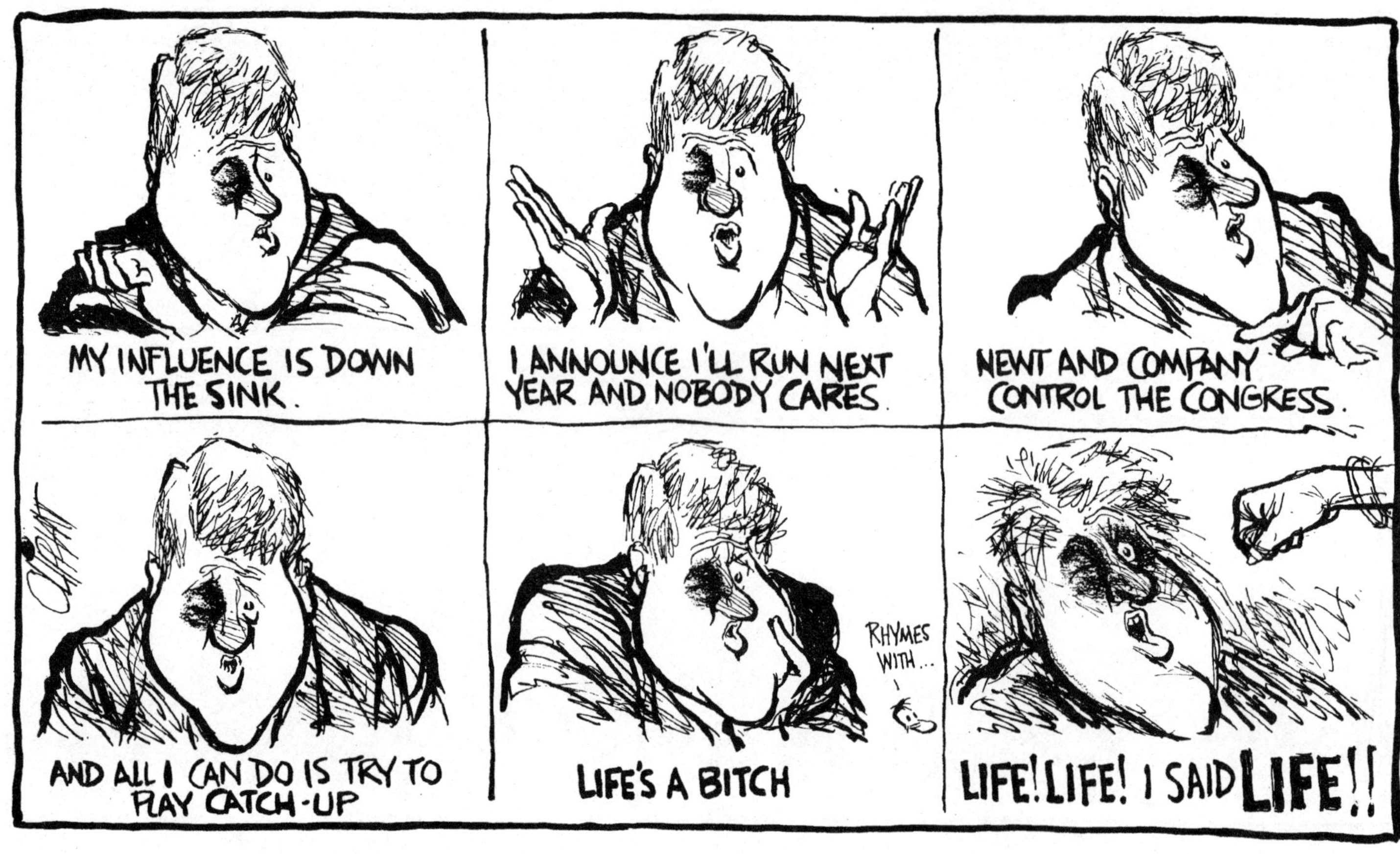
MY INFLUENCE IS DOWN THE SINK.
I ANNOUNCE I'LL RUN NEXT YEAR AND NOBODY CARES.
NEWT AND COMPANY CONTROL THE CONGRESS.
AND ALL I CAN DO IS TRY TO PLAY CATCH-UP
LIFE'S A BITCH
RHYMES WITH...
LIFE! LIFE! I SAID LIFE!!

January 12, 1995

BOMB 'EM BACK TO THE STONE AGE!
CHECHNYA

'I HAD TO DESTROY DEMOCRACY IN ORDER TO SAVE IT!'

January 13, 1995

PUBLIC BROAD- CASTING
NOW, THAT'S WHAT I CALL BROAD CASTING!
BROADLY SPEAKING
RUSH

'YOU COMMIE ELITISTS WILL HAVE TO LEAVE — WE'LL BE NEEDING THESE STUDIOS FOR MORE MEANINGFUL PROGRAMMING.'

January 13, 1995

NEWT'S CONTRACT WITH Y'ALL
READ IT FOR LOOPHOLES
OLIPHANT

'OF COURSE IT'S A HONEYMOON, HONEY—READ THE CONTRACT.'

January 18, 1995

BAILEY
SHAPIRO
SEND IN THE ⊙✱::!!!✱ CLOWNS!

AMERICAN JURISPRUDENCE – A WORK IN PROGRESS.

January 19, 1995

DO US A PAINTING FOR NORMAL AMERICANS
PAINT US AN ELVIS ON BLACK VELVET
SOMETHING IN ORANGE TO GO WITH THE COUCH IN THE DEN
AWWW THAT'S NICE, REAL NICE
ALL I KNOW ABOUT ART IS I KNOW WHAT YOU LIKE!

A MEETING OF THE CONSERVATIVE VISIGOTHS ADVISORY COMMITTEE ON THE ACCEPTABLE ARTS...

January 20, 1995

THE BOOK DEAL AND THE MURKY MURDOCH CONNECTION
SOME DO -AND THEN DENY THEY WERE ANYWHERE NEAR THE DITCH
"Men," says Professor Gingrich, in his civilization course, "are basically little piglets, drop 'em in a ditch, they just roll around in it."

January 21, 1995

'WE'VE REWRITTEN THE WAR WITH JAPAN — NOW I SUGGEST WE REWRITE THE HISTORY OF THE WAR WITH GERMANY FROM THE NAZI POINT OF VIEW. POOR THINGS HAVE BEEN MISUNDERSTOOD LATELY.'

January 24, 1995

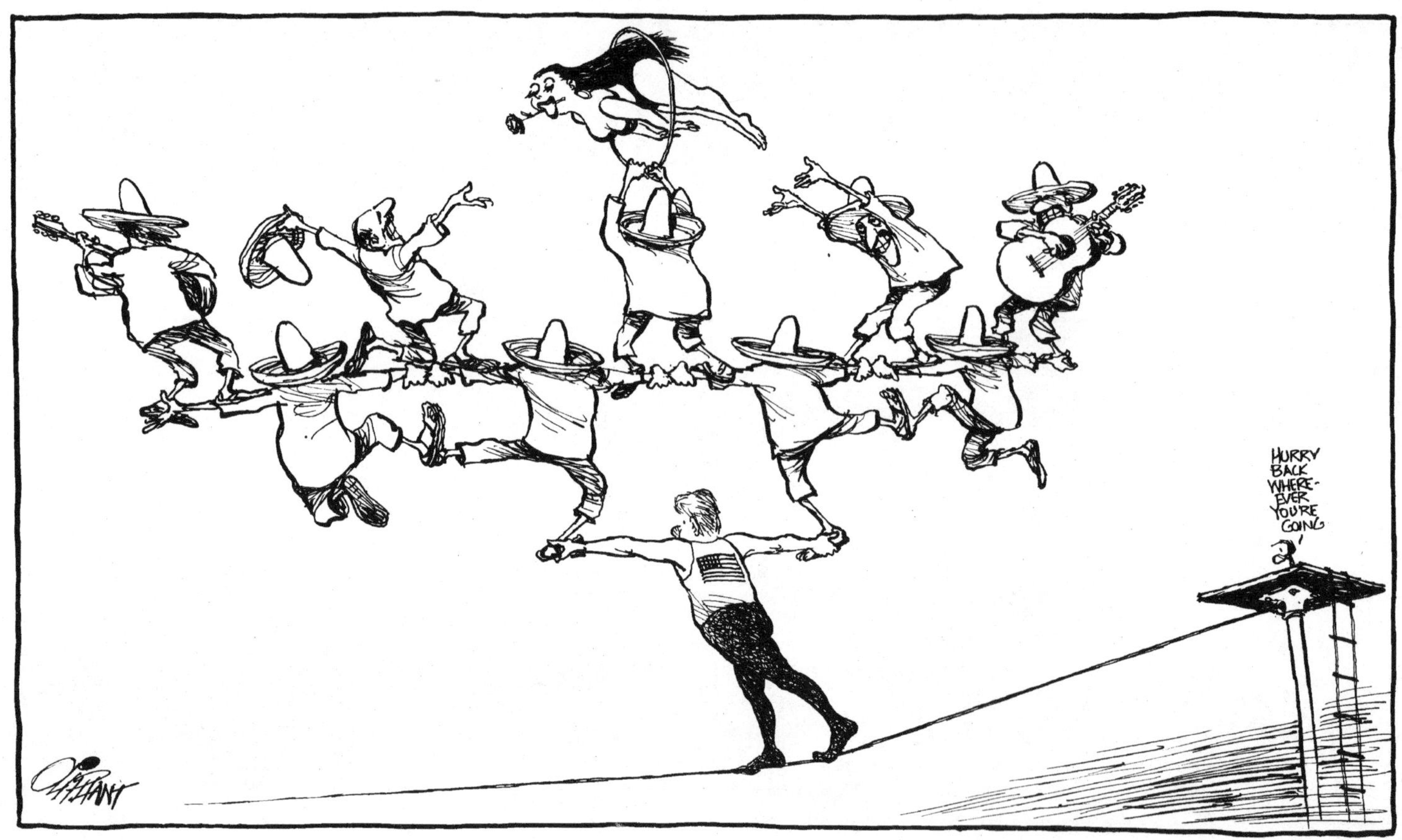
HURRY BACK WHERE-EVER YOU'RE GOING

January 25, 1995

THE FAR-REACHING EFFECTS OF THE
SIMPSON TRIAL
• HOURS WORKED DECREASE IN PROPORTION TO HOURS SPENT WATCHING TRIAL.
• PRODUCTIVITY DROPS ACCORDINGLY.
• HOUSING STARTS DOWN.
• ALAN GREENSPAN RESPONDS BY RAISING INTEREST RATES (WHAT ELSE?).
• PANICKED PRESIDENT, IN STATE OF NATION ADDRESS, BLAMES SIMPSON, LOSES SYMPATHY OF VIEWERS.
• REPUBLICANS JUBILANT. EXPECT WIN IN '96.
NATIONAL PRODUCTIVITY
HOURS WORKED
HOURS WATCHING SIMPSON TRIAL
WILLIE IN WONDERLAND

January 25, 1995

OLIPHANT
CHEZ NEWT
I BET IF WE TOOK HIS COURSE, WE'D LEARN ALL SORTS OF GREAT STUFF!
YEP— LIKE WHO'S EDUCATING TH' CHILDREN

'COOK IT YOURSELF — I'VE GOT AN INFECTION!'

February 8, 1995

CONTRACT WITH AMERICA
BUDGET '96
NOW, WE'LL SEE IF ANVILS CAN FLOAT..

February 9, 1995

YOU'RE BOTH EARNING FAR TOO MUCH – FOR THE SAKE OF THE ECONOMY I'VE NO CHOICE BUT TO RAISE YOUR INTEREST RATES IN PERPETUITY BY 50%...
OH, LOOK! YOU HAVE AN ILLEGAL ANTI-TRUST EXEMPTION – WE'LL HAVE TO DISALLOW THAT...
GREENSPAN AS ARBITRATOR!?
THIS IS ALL YOUR FILTHY, GREEDY @!!*☼! FAULT!!
OLIPHANT
OWNERS
Players

February 10, 1995

GO BACK OUT AND HAUL IN A DENTIST!
DOC FOSTER
THANKS, DR. BOOTH

THE PRESIDENT'S NOMINEE HOUND HAS SCREWED UP AGAIN.

February 11, 1995

TRAINS
POLICE
PO LICE
HOUSE APPROVES EASING RULES OF SEARCH
HIMMLER JUBILANT
AREN'T YOU SUPPOSED TO SERVE AND PROTECT?
SEARCH AND DESTRUCT, YOU MEAN.

'I'M SEARCHING YOUR POCKETS, IF IT'S ANY OF YOUR DAMN' BUSINESS.'

February 15, 1995

'WHEN YOU FINISH THAT LOST PARAKEET REPORT, MAYBE YOU CAN FIGURE WHAT TO DO WITH THESE 100,000 EXTRA OFFICERS MR. CLINTON SENT US.'

February 16, 1995

E
I
B
F
J
IS THERE A SPIN DOCTOR IN THE HOUSE?

'JUST FOR A MONTH OR SO, DR. FOSTER—GIVE THE FOLKS TIME TO FORGET ABOUT YOU.'

February 17, 1995

February 17, 1995

CHEZ NEWT
CONTRACT
OFF TO THE ORPHANAGE WITH YOU!
BOTH OF YOU!

'NOT A PENNY, YOU SHAMELESS YOUNG HUSSY— YOU SHOULD HAVE HAD AN ABORTION!'

February 22, 1995

DON'T ASK FOR CREDIT
NATIONAL
NEW HAMPSHIRE PROGRESSIVE CLUB MEETS HERE DAILY
I THOUGHT THE IDEA WAS LESS GUMMINT!
OLIPHANT

... AND A YEAR EARLY, WHAT'S MORE!

BRER BROWN
'YESSIR, 'BRER CLINTON, HIS OWNSELF, PUT ME IN CHARGE OF THIS HERE HEN HOUSE — NOW, WOULD I STEAL CHICKENS FROM OL' BRER CLINTON?'
WELL, I DUNNO— THEY'S A LOT O' FEATHERS FLOATIN' AROUND..
OLIPHANT

February 27, 1995

'LOOK AT THE BRIGHT SIDE, JOSE — AT LEAST WE DON'T LIVE IN WASHINGTON, D.C...'

February 28, 1995

BOSNIA, THE U.N., NATO, RUSSIA, MEXICO, CHINA, THE WHOLE MESS WAS TOO MUCH FOR POOR UNCLE SAM, SO HE BECAME AN ISOLATIONIST CONSERVATIVE, TOOK HIMSELF OFF TO BED, AND NEVER GOT UP AGAIN.
GUIDED TOUR STARTS HERE
SHHH

March 2, 1995

OLIPHANT
WAITING ROOM
DOCTOR SAYS YOU PROBABLY DON'T NEED THOSE ANY MORE.
AFFIRMATIVE ACTION
THEY MAY, HOWEVER, HAVE BECOME GRAFTED TO HIM!

March 3, 1995

'WE'RE SUING FOR MILLIONS – THE TOBACCO COMPANIES SHOULDA WARNED US SMOKING IS DANGEROUS!'

March 4, 1995

'I'LL BE BACK.'

March 8, 1995

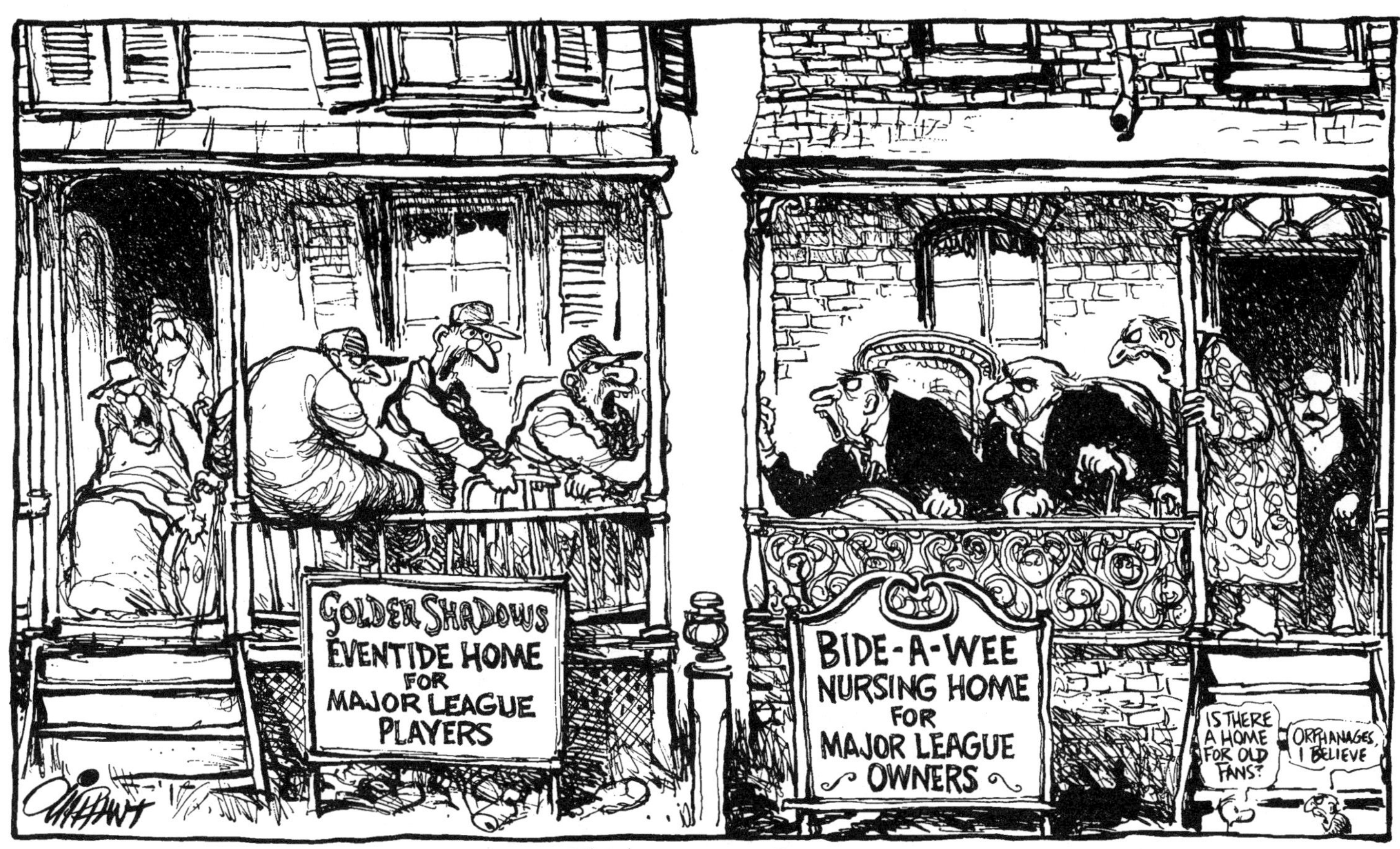
GOLDEN SHADOWS
EVENTIDE HOME
FOR
MAJOR LEAGUE
PLAYERS
BIDE-A-WEE
NURSING HOME
FOR
MAJOR LEAGUE
OWNERS
IS THERE A HOME FOR OLD FANS?
ORPHANAGES, I BELIEVE

BASEBALL, 2001.

March 11, 1995

ANYTHING THAT MAKES A LAWYER CRY, CAN'T BE ALL BAD.
HOUSE BILL WOULD LIMIT INVESTORS' LAWSUITS
Lawyers See Chilling Effect
HE COULD FILE A CLASS-ACTION SUIT
CAN THE CLASSLESS FILE CLASS ACTIONS?

March 11, 1995

I WANNA CASH IN THESE MEXICAN BONDS, IN DOLLARS
EL BANCO
SI, SEÑOR-PLEASE WAIT HERE
PLEASE, SEÑOR, LEND ME THE DOLLARS TO PAY OFF THEES FOREIGN INVESTOR!
EL GOVERNMENTO
¡CARAMBA! WAIT HERE
SPLASH
SPLASH
SEÑOR SAM-LEND ME THEES MANY DOLLARS TO LEND EL BANCO TO PAY OFF THE FOREIGN INVESTOR
WELL~ JUST A LOAN, MIND...
$
¡MUCHAS GRACIAS!
$
SPLASH
SPLASH
I'LL WAIT HERE
HAVE YOU LOOKED IN HERE, RECENTLY?-
$

March 15, 1995

THE GOOD NEWS IS HE MADE A GOOD APPOINTMENT, FOR ONCE!
THE GOOD NEWS IS OUR BOY, DEUTCH, WILL HEAD C.I.A.!
THE GOOD NEWS IS, HE'S MAKING IT A CABINET-LEVEL JOB!
THE GOOD NEWS IS, I FINALLY PLEASED SOMEBODY...
WHAT'S THE BAD NEWS?
ALL OF THE ABOVE

March 16, 1995

WHITE HOUSE PERSONNEL OFFICE
NOW HIRING
YOU WANNA BE PRESIDENT!? YOU'RE HIRED.

'YOU WANNA BE SURGEON GENERAL? YOU'RE HIRED. YOU WANNA BE HOUSING SECRETARY? YOU'RE HIRED. YOU WANNA BE SECRETARY OF COMMERCE? YOU'RE HIRED. YOU WANNA BE SECRETARY OF TRANSPORTATION?'

March 17, 1995

BANK O
MEXICO
WHEN IT COMES TO HAVES AND HAVE-NOTS, THE HAVES HAVE IT!

'DIVERSIFY.'

March 18, 1995

I'VE LOST TOUCH— WHO'S THE DEFENDANT?

AMERICAN JURISPRUDENCE (CONTINUED).

March 22, 1995

FOR THAT MONEY HE CAN BUY HIMSELF A BUNCH OF HATS!
SAY 'AAAH'

'YOUR CLAIMS OF MALPRACTICE WILL, THANK GOODNESS, BE LIMITED BY LAW TO $250,000...'

March 22, 1995

NO BELLYACHING
DURING SCHOOL EATING PERIODS
WHAT'S FOR DESSERT?
VEAL ICECREAM, BUT YOU HAVE TO EAT YOUR VEGGIE FIRST...

'CLINTON STARTS TO LOOK BETTER AND BETTER—PLEASE PASS THE VEGETABLE.'

March 23, 1995

I'M PREGNANT AGAIN— IS MY CHECK READY?
WHO'S THE FATHER?
WELFARE
HE DIDN'T SAY.
DO YOU HAVE A JOB?
WELFARE
NO.
HOW LONG HAVE YOU BEEN PREGNANT?
WELFARE
TEN MINUTES— IS MY CHECK READY?
AND YOU THINK WE NEED TO SCRAP THIS SYSTEM?
NOT A MINUTE TOO SOON!
WELFARE

JUDGE, I'D LIKE YOU TO MEET MY FRIEND, KATO KAELIN — HE'S AN ABSOLUTE RIOT!
I'M IN NEED OF A WRITER, MR. KAELIN — THINK YOU COULD DO ME SOME GOOD ONE-LINERS?
HEY, CALL ME KATO — OR CALL ME A CAB — BUT SERIOUSLY, JUDGE, LEMME WORK ON IT. WE COULD DO LUNCH. I'LL GIVE YOU MY AGENT'S NUMBER...
..SO THE SHARK SAYS, "IT'S JUST PROFESSIONAL COURTESY!" I DON'T GET IT.
LAWYER JOKES
IF YOU WANT TO BUILD A ZONKER FROM THE GROUND UP, THIS IS A SET OF PLANS!
OLIPHANT

AMERICAN JURISPRUDENCE (CONTINUED).

March 29, 1995

WE DON'T, OF COURSE, DO THAT...
...PHEW! (AHEM) SORT OF THING ANY MORE.
NOT THAT YOU EVER DID, MIND
OLIPHANT

March 30, 1995

GINGRICH $4.5M BOOK CONTRACT
THINGS ARE USUALLY WHAT THEY SEEM

'I KNOW WHAT YOU ETHICS COMMITTEE PEOPLE ARE THINKING, AND YOU SHOULD BE ASHAMED OF YOURSELVES — MR. MURDOCH AND I HARDLY KNOW EACH OTHER!'

March 31, 1995

MAGIC TERM-LIMITS MACHINE & VOTING BOOTH
TERRIFIC! YOU WIND IT UP AND IT KICKS THE BUMS OUT!

April 1, 1995

WHERE DID THE FLOWERS COME FROM?
YOU DON'T ASK, I WON'T TELL
POLICY OVER-TURNED

'YOO-HOO, GENERAL — I'M BAAA-A-CK!'

April 4, 1995

IONAIRES ONLY
PLAYERS
TICKETS
ADMISSION $6.50 PAY UP & SHUT UP
LET'S GO WATCH THE BUMS ON TV!
OR NOT!

April 5, 1995

PAPAL ENCYCLICAL
WE RECYCLE ENCYCLICALS
"IT'S ALL ON THE VALUE AND INVIOLABILITY OF HUMAN LIFE — FORTUNATELY, CHOIRBOYS ARE NOT MENTIONED."

April 6, 1995

PENTAGON PORK
HOW COME THE PIG HAS A WOODEN LEG?
WHY, HE'S BEEN AROUND SO LONG, HE'S SORTA MY FAVORITE PIG— I JUST COULDN'T BEAR TO EAT HIM ALL AT ONCE!
KINDA LIKE FAMILY
CONGRESS

ENCOURAGED TO ESTABLISH THEIR OWN SOPHISTICATED JUSTICE SYSTEMS, THIRD WORLD PEOPLES ARE EXTRACTING VALUABLE LESSONS FROM THEIR OBSERVATIONS OF THE O.J. SIMPSON SHOW.
HUH?
WHAT MEANS IT? EXPLAIN IT TO US, O, WISE ONE.
THE LESSON IS OBVIOUS— MY SON MUST BECOME A LAWYER!
THE ROT IS NOW COMPLETE

April 19, 1995

AWW, DON'T CRY, SECRETARY McNAMARA — YOUR NAME AIN'T UP THERE.
WELL, HECK — EVEN WAR CRIMINALS GET THE BLUES

April 21, 1995

DEAR MR. CLINTON: JUST BECAUSE WE BOMBED OKLAHOMA CITY IS NO REASON TO CALL US "EVIL COWARDS." YOU HAVE HURT OUR FEELINGS. WE DEMAND AN APOLOGY.

April 22, 1995

WHAT TA' HECK -HE'S GOING TO WALK, ANYWAY...
I COULDN'T FIGURE WHAT WAS HAPPENING BACK THERE, O.J.
YEAH, I DON'T THINK THEY'LL EVER MISS US, JUDGE.

AMERICAN JURISPRUDENCE (CONTINUED).

April 26, 1995

CRAZIES
F.B.I.
UNLIMITED
IS THERE A "NONE OF THE ABOVE"?

April 27, 1995

OLIPHANT
RUSH
OLLIE
G. GORDON
WELCOME TO THE RESPONSIBLE FRINGE

'WE MUST BE RESPONSIBLE IN USING OUR FREEDOM OF EXPRESSION, SKINHEAD.' 'TRUE, LARDBODY—WE WOULD NOT WANT TO STIR UP THE IDIOT FRINGE.'

April 28, 1995

McNAMARA IS RIGHT... VE VERE WRONG ABOUD DER VIETNAM VOR— DERRIBLY WRONG!
McNAMARA'S MEA CULPA
30 YEARS LATE AND A FEW DOLLARS SHORT
I DIDN'T KNOW HENRY DID MEA CULPA
HENRY DOES "YOU-A CULPA", OR "WHO-A, MEA CULPA?"

DON'T HOLD YOUR BREATH FOR THIS ONE...

April 29, 1995

MAYBE YOU SHOULD WORK ON YOUR CAMOUFLAGE, SIR...

"YOU MAY BE THE COMMANDING GENERAL OF POST 17 OF THE GRAND PATRIOT MILITIA, BUT IN THIS OUTFIT YOU'RE THE PRIVATE WHO TAKES THE GARBAGE TO THE DUMP!"

May 3, 1995

HOW'S THAT AGAIN ABOUT MEDICARE, SONNY?
NOTHING, NOTHING -
THE LOOPHOLES, DAMMIT, THERE'S GOTTA BE LOOPHOLES!
CONTRACT
A BALANCED BUDGET GUARANTEE NO MATTER WHAT
WHEREAS
WHEREBY
WHEREFORE
HEREINAFTER
WHYFORE
AFORESAID
GRAMMAW PACKS A WALLOP
STILL

May 4, 1995

MR. CLINTON'S FIRST SURGEON GENERAL GOT RUN OFF BECAUSE SHE MENTIONED MASTURBATION.
HEY, THERE'S A WORD I NEVER THOUGHT I'D SEE IN A CARTOON
NOW THERE ARE REPUBLICANS ON THE HILL WHO WOULD MAKE ABORTION THE ISSUE TO DEFEAT DR. FOSTER'S NOMINATION.
UM
THERE'D BE NONE OF THIS NONSENSE IF THE RELIGIOUS RIGHT WOULD JUST SEEK TO BAN ALL SEX COMPLETELY!
SHHH - THEY'LL HEAR YOU!
ALL THEY'D NEED TO DO IS BULLY IT THROUGH THE SENATE
I'M SELLING MY CONDOM STOCK

May 5, 1995

OLIPHANT
CHEZ LIDDY
I DIDN'T KNOW CONVICTED FELONS WERE ALLOWED TO OWN GUNS..
U.S. POSTAL SERVICE

'HEAD SHOT! HEAD SHOT! GOT THE NO-GOOD, JACKBOOTED, GOVERNMENT SUMBITCH!'

May 6, 1995

WHAT IS THE SOUND OF NO HANDS CLAPPING?
OLIPHANT

BASEBALL PHILOSOPHY PUZZLE: IF A BALL IS HIT INTO EMPTY STANDS, DOES IT MAKE A SOUND?

May 10, 1995

CONGRATULATIONS— I'M STILL HERE.
V·E
1945
ON TO V·J DAY!
OLIPHANT

May 11, 1995

FBI
OLIPHANT
PEOPLE ARE THINKING OF US AS A BUNCH OF OUT-OF-CONTROL CROSS-DRESSING FASCISTS!
YOU MEAN YOU'RE NOT?

'I WAS ABOUT TO SAY THAT IF OL' J. EDGAR WAS STILL RUNNING THINGS, WE WOULDN'T BE HAVING THIS BIG IMAGE PROBLEM... BUT LET IT PASS.'

May 11, 1995

OLIPHANT
MOSCOW SUMMIT
NATO
EXPANSION
TRY TAKING THE SHOES OFF

'HEY, BORIS — WHERE DO WE START?'

May 12, 1995

WELL, GOL-LEE! — WHERE'D EVVERBODY GO?
THEY JUST MELTED AWAY INTO THE SCENERY— WRAITH-LIKE, THEY WAS...
CRACK TROOPS OF THE FIRST DOGBERRY MILITIA TRAINING TO FOIL THE ENEMY BY SLIPPING INTO THE FOREST, SILENT AND UNSEEN.